North Carolina

The Tar Heel State

Jason Glaser

PowerKiDS press™

New York

To my daughter, Mira. I hope to have some livermush and grape jelly with you some day.

Published in 2010 by The Rosen Publishing Group, Inc.
29 East 21st Street, New York, NY 10010

First Edition

3 1350 00292 5511

Editor: Amelie von Zumbusch
Book Design: Greg Tucker
Photo Researcher: Jessica Gerweck

Photo Credits: Cover Bill Losh/Getty Images; pp. 5, 7, 22 (tree), 22 (mammal), 22 (flag), 22 (flower) Shutterstock.com; pp. 9, 22 (James Polk) MPI/Getty Images; p. 11 © Adam Jones/Corbis; p. 13 Steve Hopkin/Getty Images; p. 15 © Superstock/age fotostock; p. 17 Don Klumpp/Getty Images; p. 19 © A.H.C./age fotostock; p. 22 (bird) © www.iStockphoto.com /Tony Cambell; p. 22 (Dolley Madison) Stock Montage/Getty Images; p. 22 (Dale Earnhardt Jr.) Ezra Shaw/Getty Images for NASCAR.

Library of Congress Cataloging-in-Publication Data

Glaser, Jason.
  North Carolina : the Tar Heel State / Jason Glaser. — 1st ed.
      p. cm. — (Our amazing states)
  Includes index.
  ISBN 978-1-4358-9394-8 (library binding) — ISBN 978-1-4358-9780-9 (pbk.) —
ISBN 978-1-4358-9781-6 (6-pack)
  1. North Carolina—Juvenile literature. I. Title.
  F254.3.G536 2010
  975.6—dc22

                                        2009027402

Manufactured in the United States of America

CPSIA Compliance Information: Batch #WW10PK: For Further Information contact Rosen Publishing; New York, New York at 1-800-237-9932

Contents

Ever-Changing Shores

Life in North Carolina is a continuous mix of **tradition** and change. The state is known for both historic **sites** and cutting-edge **research**. This state lies along the Atlantic Ocean. It shares borders with Virginia, South Carolina, Georgia, and Tennessee.

North Carolina's Outer Banks are a good example of the way things in North Carolina can change and yet stay the same. People have visited and lived on these islands for centuries. However, the boat captains who carry people back and forth to the warm beaches must always look for how the islands and waters are changing. Each storm reshapes the sand and waterways. North Carolinians have built lighthouses to guide ships through these changing waters.

Storms are always reshaping the islands of North Carolina's Outer Banks. In this picture, you can see how storms have piled up sand on a beach in the Outer Banks.

Getting Started in a New World

The first British **colony** in North America was at Roanoke Island, in what is now North Carolina. One of the colony's leaders left to get supplies. When he returned, everyone was gone! People think the colonists may have moved to Croatoan Island to live with Native Americans, but no one knows.

In time, other British settlers arrived. In 1663, the colony of Carolina was formed. The northern part of the colony was hard to reach by boat. The colonists there often felt cut off from the outside world. They had different problems and beliefs about government than colonists in southern Carolina did. By the time the American colonists broke free from Great Britain in the **American Revolution**, North Carolina and South Carolina had become different colonies.

Tryon Palace, seen here, was rebuilt in the 1950s. The grand house was home to the governor of North Carolina when it was a colony.

Building and Rebuilding the State

During the American Revolution, North Carolina soldiers became known for their bravery. They stayed in battle when others ran away. One joke said that the soldiers must have tar from North Carolina pine trees stuck to their feet and that their "tar heels" held them in place. North Carolina, the Tar Heel State, joined the United States in November 1789.

North Carolina grew quickly, and settlers forced the Native Americans out. A small group hid, and those Cherokees still live in North Carolina today. In 1861, North Carolina joined the Southern states during the Civil War to fight for states' rights and **slavery**. The South lost the war, and North Carolina lost many soldiers. A second wave of settlers from the North soon came to rebuild.

Wilmington, North Carolina, was a key port for the South during the Civil War. Here, Southern soldiers are shown guarding Wilmington's Fort Fisher.

Warm with a Chance of Rain

The land and the weather in North Carolina are different depending on where you are. The tall Appalachian Mountains, in the western part of the state, get plenty of rain in summer and snow in winter. The coastal plain, in eastern North Carolina, is flat land. It has many rivers and swamps. Temperatures are mild there most of the year. The hills and forests of the Piedmont lie between the mountains and the coastal plain.

Off the state's coast are the Outer Banks. This set of sandy islands keeps the state safe from strong winds and storms. Sometimes **hurricanes** break through to the mainland, but they lose a lot of power while they are crossing the Outer Banks.

North Carolina's Pisgah National Forest offers beautiful views of the Appalachian Mountains. In the fall, you can see many colorful trees there.

Filled with Forests

Forests reach across North Carolina. Deer, black bears, and **endangered** red wolves pass through rows of Fraser fir. Wild animals also live among pine trees. These evergreens are the state tree. The flowers of the dogwood tree are the state flower. Spanish moss, which is not really moss, hangs off oak and cypress trees in the Great Dismal Swamp, while snakes and alligators creep beneath.

North Carolina is home to several kinds of Venus flytraps. The Venus flytrap is the state's **carnivorous** plant. The plant has traps at the ends of its leaves. When a bug lands on a plant's trap, it closes and eats the bug! Flytraps are fun to watch, but do not pick them. They are **protected** in North Carolina.

Venus flytraps generally grow in poor soil. The plants cannot get everything they need to grow from the soil, so they trap bugs to get the other nutrients they need.

Looking past Cotton and Tobacco

North Carolinians used to say that cotton and tobacco were king. This meant that they were the most important things the state produced. Today, North Carolina still sells cotton goods and tobacco. Farmers here are also among the country's top sellers of pigs and chickens.

North Carolina has also moved into other businesses. The state set aside land called Research Triangle Park, where companies build places to study and produce new things. Several banks and big companies are based in Charlotte, North Carolina. Many movie and television crews make their shows in North Carolina. The sights that their cameras capture also draw many visitors to North Carolina every year.

Piedmont Triad Research Park is in Winston-Salem, North Carolina. It is home to companies that discover new ideas in health, science, and computer systems.

Raleigh and Charlotte

The capital city of North Carolina, Raleigh, is named for Sir Walter Raleigh. Raleigh was the man who gave the money to start the colony at Roanoke. To remember history, the city of Raleigh holds plays in which actors dress and act as people did long ago. They sometimes pretend it is the first Independence Day, July 4, 1776. Actors also tell the story of slaves who tried to sail a slave ship, *La Amistad*, back to Africa.

Charlotte has the most people of any North Carolina city. It also feels like it has the most plants! Special gardens in Charlotte will let you see Venus flytraps, rain forest trees, and colorful flowers. Other gardens are home to hundreds of birds or butterflies.

Raleigh, seen here, is one of the fastest-growing cities in the United States. Today, the city is home to more than one million people.

Wright Takes Flight

In 1900, brothers Wilbur and Orville Wright picked the Outer Banks of North Carolina for something very special. These two bike makers wanted to build the very first airplane. For three years, they caught the ocean winds in kitelike wings and crashed down again in the soft sand of Kitty Hawk, North Carolina. On December 17, 1903, the brothers got their plane to fly 120 feet (37 m) in 12 seconds with Orville inside.

Today, you can go to the Wright Brothers National Memorial at Kitty Hawk. There, you can see a model of the Wright brothers' plane. You can stand where that first flight happened. Kids who visit there can even build paper airplanes of their own!

Here, you can see the plane in which Orville Wright made his historic flight. The flight took place at 10:35 in the morning on a cold and windy day.

So Much to Find

There are many stories about the **pirate** Blackbeard, who often sailed in the waters near North Carolina. Blackbeard died in a battle near the state's Ocracoke Island and his ship was sunk. His ship was later found, but his **treasure** never was. Today, people still go to North Carolina looking for Blackbeard's treasure.

Even if travelers visiting North Carolina do not find pirate gold, they can always find friendly people and lots to do. Visitors can try tasty treasures, such as seafood from Calabash, **barbecue** from Lexington, and **livermush** from Shelby. These North Carolina cities are known all across the country for these foods. Once you have eaten a few bites, you will see why North Carolinians smile so much!

Glossary

American Revolution (uh-MER-uh-ken reh-vuh-LOO-shun) Battles that soldiers from the colonies fought against Britain for freedom, from 1775 to 1783.

barbecue (BAHR-bih-kyoo) Food cooked outside on a grill, over an open fire, or over hot coals or wood.

carnivorous (kahr-NIH-vuh-rus) Eating animals.

colony (KAH-luh-nee) A new place where people move that is still ruled by the leaders of the country from which they came.

endangered (in-DAYN-jerd) In danger of no longer living.

hurricanes (HUR-ih-kaynz) Storms with strong winds and heavy rain.

livermush (LIH-ver-muhsh) A dish made from pig meat and ground corn.

pirate (PY-rut) A person who attacks and robs ships.

protected (pruh-TEK-ted) Kept safe.

research (rih-SERCH) Careful study.

sites (SYTS) Places where certain events happened.

slavery (SLAY-vuh-ree) The system of one person "owning" another.

tradition (truh-DIH-shun) A way of doing something that has been passed down over time.

treasure (TREH-zher) A group of things of great worth or value.

North Carolina State Symbols

**State Tree
Pine Tree**

**State Mammal
Gray Squirrel**

State Flag

**State Bird
Cardinal**

**State Flower
Dogwood**

State Seal

Famous People from North Carolina

Dolley Madison
(1768–1849)
Born in
Guilford County, NC
First Lady

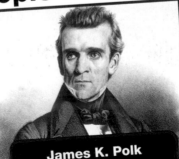

James K. Polk
(1795–1849)
Born in Mecklenburg
County, NC
U.S. President

Dale Earnhardt, Jr.
(1974–)
Born in Concord, NC
NASCAR Driver

North Carolina State Map

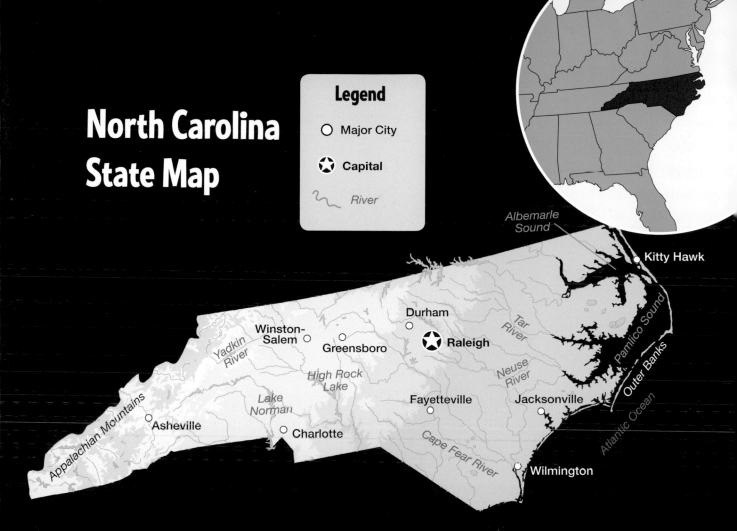

Legend

○ Major City

✪ Capital

〜 River

Albemarle Sound

Kitty Hawk

Durham

Tar River

Winston-Salem

Greensboro

✪ Raleigh

Yadkin River

High Rock Lake

Neuse River

Pamlico Sound

Outer Banks

Lake Norman

Fayetteville

Jacksonville

Atlantic Ocean

Appalachian Mountains

Asheville

Charlotte

Cape Fear River

Wilmington

North Carolina State Facts

Population: About 8,049,313

Area: 52,669 square miles (136,412 sq km)

Motto: "Esse Quam Videri" ("To be, rather than to seem")

Song: "The Old North State," written and arranged by William Gaston

Index

A
American Revolution, 6, 8

B
barbecue, 20
beaches, 4
boat captains, 4
borders, 4

C
Civil War, 8
colony, 6, 16

D
deer, 12

G
Georgia, 4

H
historic sites, 4
hurricanes, 10

I
island(s), 4, 6, 10, 20

L
livermush, 20

O
Outer Banks, 4, 10, 18

P
people, 4, 6, 16, 20

R
research, 4

S
sand, 4, 18
slavery, 8
South Carolina, 4, 6
storm(s), 4, 10

T
Tennessee, 4
treasure(s), 20

V
Venus flytrap(s), 12, 16
Virginia, 4

W
waters, 4, 20
waterways, 4

Web Sites

Due to the changing nature of Internet links, PowerKids Press has developed an online list of Web sites related to the subject of this book. This site is updated regularly. Please use this link to access the list:

www.powerkidslinks.com/amst/nc/